THOUGHTS FOR YOUNG MEN

*An Exhortation Directed to
Those in the Prime of Life*

J C RYLE

LIGHTLY EDITED & UPDATED BY MARY DAVIS

EP BOOKS

Unit C, Tomlinson Road, Leyland, PR25 2DY

Email: epbooks@10ofthose.com

© EP Books 2018

This edition first published 2018

Reprinted 2021

British Library Cataloguing in Publication Data available

ISBN 978–1–78397–218–0

THOUGHTS FOR YOUNG MEN

*An Exhortation Directed to
Those in the Prime of Life*

CONTENTS

THOUGHTS FOR YOUNG MEN

'Likewise, urge the younger men to be self-controlled.'
Titus 2:6

When Paul wrote his letter to Titus about his duties as a minister, he mentioned young men as needing particular attention and encouragement. After speaking about older men and older women, and then younger women, Paul adds this pithy piece of advice: 'Likewise, urge the younger men to be self-controlled.'[1] I am going to follow the apostle's advice. I want to offer a few words of friendly encouragement to young men.

I am growing old myself, but I remember my days as a young man so well. I have most vivid memories of the joys and the sorrows, the hopes and the fears, the temptations and the difficulties, the mistaken judgments and the misplaced affections, the failures and the ambitions that go with being a young man. If I can say something which helps just one young man go in the right direction, and saves him from faults and sins which may ruin his prospects for both this life and eternity, I shall be very thankful.

In this short book, there are four things I want to do:

- I will mention some *reasons* why young men need encouragement

- I will point out some special *dangers* which young men need to be warned about

- I will offer some *advice* which I beg young men to take seriously

- I will suggest some *rules* which I strongly advise young men to follow

I have something to say on each of these four points, and I pray that what I say may be useful to some people.

I. REASONS FOR ENCOURAGING YOUNG MEN

In the first place, what are the reasons that young men need special encouragement? I will mention several.

FEW YOUNG MEN SEEM TO HAVE REAL CHRISTIAN FAITH

For one thing, there is the painful fact that very few young men seem to have real Christian faith. I am not pointing the finger at a particular kind of young man; I speak of all young men. High-born or low, rich or poor, sophisticated or unsophisticated, educated or uneducated, in the city or the countryside—it makes no difference. I tremble to see how few young men are genuinely led by the Holy Spirit, how few of them walk in the narrow way which leads to eternal life, how few are setting their hearts on the Lord and on things above, how few are taking up their cross and following Christ. I say this with a heavy heart but, before God, I do believe I am saying nothing more than the truth.

Young men, you form a large and important part of the population of this country. But, I ask you, where and in what condition are your immortal souls? I fear that wherever we turn, the answer is the same.

What would any faithful *church ministers* say about this? How many unmarried young people can he count on to be at the Lord's Supper? Who is slowest to take advantage about the 'means of grace': the most sporadic about being at Sunday services; the most difficult to get to weekly bible studies and prayer meetings; the most inattentive to preaching and sermons? Which part of his congregation fills him with most anxiety? Who are the ones that cause him most anguish and heart-searching? Who in his flock are the hardest to manage, the ones who need the most frequent warnings and rebukes? the ones who cause him the greatest uneasiness and sorrow? For whose souls is he most fearful? For whose eternal destiny is he tempted to feel most hopeless? Depend on it, his answer will almost certainly be: *the young men.*

What would *parents* have to say? Who in their families gives them most pain and trouble? Who needs the most watchfulness? Who most often vexes and disappoints them? Who are the first to be led away from what is right, and the last to remember warnings and good advice? Who are the most difficult to keep in order? the hardest to convince that they should observe boundaries? Who most frequently falls into open sin, disgraces the name of Christ, makes their friends unhappy, and saddens elderly relations? Who brings their parents' 'gray hair with sorrow to the grave'?[2] Depend on it, the answer will generally be: *the young men.*

How about *those in authority*? Who goes to public houses and beer-shops most? Who are the ones taking part in gangs and riots? Who are most often in trouble with the law—for drunkenness, breaches of the peace, fighting, stealing, assaults and other criminal behaviour? Who fills the jails and youth offending centres? Who in our society needs most careful watching and looking after? You can be sure that they will point to the same group: *the young men.*

How about *wealthy families*? We might think that great wealth would do away with these problems. But if we were to ask some of the richest families, we would find the same situation. In one family, we would see the sons wasting their time, health and money in the selfish pursuit of pleasure. In another, the sons will not have a proper job, and will be frittering away the most precious years of their life doing nothing of value. In another family, they may take up a profession for appearance's sake, but fail to work conscientiously. In another, they are always making unhelpful friendships, gambling, getting into debts, mixing with 'the wrong sort', keeping their friends in a fever-pitch of anxiety. I'm afraid that rank, title, wealth and education do not prevent these things! Anxious fathers, heart-broken mothers, and sorrowing sisters could tell sad tales about them, if the truth were known. Many a family, with everything this world can give, has a relation who is never talked about, or perhaps talked about with regret and shame. Some son, some brother, some cousin, some nephew—who has had things all his own way, and is a grief to all who know him.

There is rarely a rich family which has not got some thorn in its side, some blot on its page of happiness, some constant source of pain and anxiety. Often, far too often, do we not discover that the true cause is this: *the young men?*

What shall we say about this? These are facts: plain staring facts, facts which meet us on every side, facts which cannot be denied. How dreadful this is! It is dreadful to think that every time I meet a young man, I meet someone who is (in all probability) an enemy of God, travelling in the broad way which leads to destruction, unfit for heaven! With these facts before me, you cannot be surprised that I think there is an issue here. You cannot be surprised that I want to encourage you!

ALL YOUNG MEN WILL FACE DEATH AND JUDGMENT

For another thing, young men, just like everyone else, will face death and judgment, and nearly all of them seem to forget this.

Young men, let me say this to you: you are destined to die once, and after that to face judgment.[3] However strong and healthy you are now, the day of your death may actually be very near. I see young people who are sick, as well as old. I bury youthful corpses, as well as old ones. I read the names of people no older than you in every churchyard. I learn from books that, apart from infancy

---

3   Heb 9:27

and old age, more die between the ages of thirteen and twenty-three than at any other time of life. And yet you live as though you are sure that you are never going to die!

Are you thinking that you will deal with these things *tomorrow*? Remember the words of Solomon: 'Do not boast about tomorrow, for you do not know what a day may bring'.[4] 'Serious things tomorrow!' said General Archias of the ancient city of Thebes to the man who tried to warn him of a plot to kill him the very next day.[5] 'Serious things tomorrow!' he said; but his tomorrow never came.

Tomorrow is the devil's day, but today is God's. Satan does not care how spiritual your intentions are, or how holy your resolutions might be, so long as they are fixed for tomorrow. Do not let the devil mislead you! Answer him, 'No, Satan! It shall be today. Today!' Not all men live to a ripe old age like Isaac and Jacob. Many children die before their fathers. David had to mourn the death of his two finest sons; Job lost all his ten children in one day. Your experience may be like one of theirs. When death summons, it will be useless to talk of tomorrow—you will have to go at once.

Do you think there will be *a better time* to sort these things out? Later? The road that leads to eternal separation from God is paved with such thoughts. Better to sort it out now while you can. Leave nothing unsettled that is eternal. Run no risk when your soul is at stake. Believe me, the salvation of a soul is not an

---

4   Prov 27:1

5   Greek biographer, Plutarch tells the story of a plot by Pelopidas to kill Archias, general of the ancient Greek city of Thebes. Archias put off reading a letter that would have alerted him of Pelopidas' plan to kill him the next day.

easy matter. We all need a 'great' salvation, whether we are young
or old. We all need to be born again. We all need to be washed
in Christ's blood. We all need to be sanctified by the Spirit. The
one who is truly happy person is the one who does not leave these
things unsettled and uncertain; the one who does not rest until he
has the witness of the Holy Spirit within him, assuring him that
he is a child of God.

Young men, your time is short. Your days are not long. They
are a shadow, a mist, a tale that is soon told. Your bodies are not
indestructible. As Isaiah says, 'Even youths shall faint and be wea-
ry, and young men shall fall exhausted.'[6] Your health may be taken
from you in a moment: it only needs a fall, a fever, an inflamma-
tion, a broken blood vessel – and your body would soon be in
the grave. There is but a step between any one of you and death.
This very night, your life might be demanded from you.[7] You are
quickly going the way of all the earth; you will soon be gone. Your
life is all uncertainty; your death and judgment are perfectly sure.
You too will stand before the 'great white throne' of God.[8] You too
must obey God's summons which Jerome the theologian says was
constantly ringing in his ears: 'Arise, ye dead, and come to judgment.'[9] 'Look, I am coming soon!' says Jesus. This is the language
of the Judge himself.[10] I cannot, I dare not, I will not leave you be.

---

6   Isaiah 40:30
7   Luke 12:20
8   Rev 20:11
9   Jerome (345-420 AD) was a bible translator and advocate of
monasticism.
10   Rev 22:7

Please take to heart these words of the Preacher from the book of Ecclesiastes:

> *'Rejoice, O young man, in your youth, and let your heart cheer you in the days of your youth. Walk in the ways of your heart and the sight of your eyes. But know that for all these things God will bring you into judgment.'*[11]

It is incredible, that faced with such a prospect, any man can be careless and unconcerned! What could be more insane than being content to live unprepared to die? What could be more extraordinary than the unbelief of men? It is no surprise that one of the clearest prophecies in the Bible begins like this, 'Who has believed what he has heard from us?'[12] It is no surprise that the Lord Jesus says, 'when the Son of Man comes, will he find faith on earth?'[13] Young men, I worry that the report on many of you in the courts above will be this: 'They will not believe.' I worry that you may be hurried out of the world, and awake to find out—too late—that death and judgment are realities.

I fear all of this – and therefore I urge you to take it to heart.

HOW YOUNG MEN TURN OUT DEPENDS LARGELY ON WHAT THEY ARE NOW

Another reason I want to encourage you is this: what young men *will be*, in all probability, depends on what they *are now*. Young men seem to forget this. Youth is the seedtime of old age, the sea-

---

11   Ecclesiastes 11:9
12   Isa 53:1
13   Luke 18:8

son of moulding and becoming in the short space of a human life, the turning point in the story of a man's mind.

By the shoot, we judge how the tree will turn out; by the blossoms, the fruit; by the spring, we assess the coming harvest; by the morning, the coming day; and by the character of the young man, we may generally judge what he will be when he grows up.

Young men, do not be deceived. Do not think you can indulge your lusts and pleasures just as you choose when you are young, and then go and serve God with ease later on. Do not think that you can live the life of a sinner, and then die the death of a saint. It is a mockery to deal with God and your soul in such a way as that. It is an awful mockery to suppose you can give the flower of your strength to the world and the devil, and then fob off the King of kings with the scraps and remains of your heart, the shipwreck and leftovers of your powers. It is an awful mockery, and you may find to your cost that it cannot be done.

Perhaps you are relying on a *late repentance*. If so, you do not know what you are trying to do. You are failing to take God into account. Repentance and faith are the *gifts* of God; gifts that he often withholds when they have been offered in vain for so long. I agree that true repentance is never too late. But, at the same time, I warn you that late repentance seldom happens. I agree that one penitent thief was converted in his final hours so that no-one might despair. But, at the same time, I warn you that *only one* was converted, that no-one might be presumptuous. I agree that the Bible says that Jesus is 'he is able to save to the uttermost those who draw near to God through him.'[14] But, at the same time, I warn you that it is also written by the same Spirit, 'Because I have called and you refused to listen,... I also will laugh at your calamity; I will mock when terror strikes you.'[15]

Believe me, you will find it no easy matter to turn to God just when you please. Archbishop Leighton was right when he said: 'The way of sin is downhill. A man cannot stop when he would.' Holy desires and serious convictions are not like a servant, always ready to come and go at your command.[16] They are more like the stubborn wild ox in the book of Job; they will not obey your voice, nor do your bidding. It was said of the famous general, Hannibal, when he *could* have conquered Rome, he chose not to; but, later, when he *wanted* to conquer it, he could not. Beware, in case the same kind of thing happens to you in the matter of eternal life.

Why do I say all this? I say it because *habits are hard to break*. I say it because experience tells me that people's hearts are seldom changed if they are not changed when they are young. Men are rarely converted when they are old. Habits have long roots. If sin is allowed to make its home in your heart, it will not be evicted at your command. Habit becomes second nature; and its chains are like a 'a threefold cord (which) is not quickly broken'.[17] The prophet Jeremiah is right when he says, 'Can the Ethiopian change his skin or the leopard his spots? Then also you can do good

---

14   Hebrews 7:25
15   Prov 1:24, 26
16   Matt 8:5
17   Ecclesiastes 4:12

who are accustomed to do evil.'[18] Habits are like stones rolling downhill: the further they roll, the faster they go and the more out-of-control they are. Habits, like trees, are strengthened by age. A child can bend an oak when it is still a young sapling; but a hundred men cannot root it up when it is a full-grown tree. A child can wade over the River Thames at its source; but the largest ship in the world can float in it when it gets near the sea. It is the same with habits: the older they are, the stronger they will be; the longer they have held possession, the harder they will be to cast out. *They* grow with our growth; they strengthen with our strength. Habit breeds sin. Each fresh act of sin lessens fear and remorse, it hardens our hearts, it blunts our conscience, and increases our evil inclinations.

Young men, you may feel that I am putting too much emphasis on this point. If you had seen old men on the brink of death, as I have—and seen how cold-hearted, callous, hard as rock they can be—you would not accuse me of exaggerating. Believe me, you cannot stand still when it comes to your soul. Habits of good or habits of evil are growing stronger in your heart each day. Every day you are either getting nearer to God, or further away. Every year that you continue to be unrepentant, the wall of division between you and heaven becomes higher and thicker; the gulf to be crossed becomes deeper and broader. Be afraid of the hardening effect of lingering in sin day after day! Now is the time to do something about it. Make sure that your flight from sin is not in the 'winter' of your days; do not put if off it until you are old. If

---

18   Jeremiah 13:23

you do not seek the Lord when you are young, the strength of habit is such that you will probably never seek him at all.

I fear this, and therefore I exhort you.

THE DEVIL IS PARTICULARLY KEEN TO DESTROY THE SOULS OF YOUNG MEN

For another thing, the devil is especially zealous in his attempts to destroy the souls of young men, and they do not seem to realise this. Satan knows very well that you can play a very significant part in the next generation, and therefore he uses every trick in the book to make you his own. I do not want you to be ignorant of his ways.

He tries out some of his best tricks and temptations on you. He spreads his net with the greatest care in order to entangle your hearts. He sets a trap and baits it with the sweetest promises to get you into his power. He displays his wars before your eyes with the utmost ingenuity in order to make you buy his sugared poisons, and eat his wretched delicacies. You are the grand focus of his attack. May the Lord rebuke him; and deliver you out of his hands.

Young men, beware of being taken by the devil's snares. He will try to throw dust in your eyes, and prevent you seeing anything in its true colours. He delights in making you think that evil is good, and good is evil.[19] He will disguise and dress up sin to make you fall in love with it.[20] He will distort, misrepresent

---

19   Isaiah 5:20
20   2 Corinthians 11:15

and caricature true faith to make you dislike it. He will exaggerate the pleasures of wickedness – but hide the sting. He will lift up before your eyes the cross and its painfulness – but keep the eternal crown out of sight. He will promise you everything if you will only serve him – just as he did to Christ.[21] He will even help you to wear a form of faith and religion, so long as you deny its power.[22] Early on in your life, he will tell you that it is too *soon* to serve God; at the end, he will tell you that it is too *late*. I beg you not to be deceived!

You do not realise the danger you are in from this enemy. And it is this ignorance which makes me fear for you. You are like blind men, walking along a road which is full of pot-holes. You do not see the dangers which are all around you.[23]

Your enemy is *mighty*. He is called 'the prince of this world' for a reason.[24] He opposed our Lord Jesus Christ all through his ministry. He tempted Adam and Eve to eat the forbidden fruit, and so brought sin and death into the world.[25] He even managed to tempt David, the 'man after God's own heart' and caused his later years to be full of sorrow.[26] He tempted even Peter, the chosen apostle, and made him deny his Lord.[27] We cannot—we must not—underestimate his hostility.

---

21   Matthew 4:8
22   2 Timothy 3:5
23   Luke 6:39
24   John 14:30
25   Genesis 3
26   2 Samuel 11:2ff
27   Matt 26:69

Your enemy is *restless*. He never sleeps. He is always going about like a roaring lion, looking for someone to devour.[28] He is forever roaming throughout the earth, and going to and fro in it.[29] You may be careless about your souls, but he is not. He wants to make them miserable, like himself, and will have your souls if he can. We cannot—we must not—underestimate his hostility.

And your enemy is *cunning*. For thousands of years, he has been reading the one book and that book is the heart of man. He ought to know it well by now, and he does know it—all its weakness, all its deceitfulness, all its folly. And he has a store of temptations which are most likely to do it harm. You will never find a place where he will not find you. Go into towns and he will be there. Go into a wilderness, he will be there also. Sit among the party goers and drunkards and he will be there to help you. Listen to preaching, and he will be there to distract you. We cannot—we must not—underestimate his hostility.

Young men, this enemy is working hard to achieve your destruction, whether you believe it or not. You are the prize he is competing for. He realises that you will either be a blessing or a curse to your generation, and he is trying hard to create a blockage in your heart early on, so that you may help forward his kingdom at some stage. He totally understands that spoiling the bud is the best way to damage the flower. I long that God should open your eyes so that you can see things as they really are, just as he opened the eyes of Elisha's servant.[30] I long that you should see exactly

---

28   1 Peter 5:8

29   Job 1:7

30   2 Kings 6:13-17

what Satan is scheming in order to wreck your peace. Whether you want to hear or not, I cannot, I dare not, I will not leave you be. I must warn you; I must encourage you.

YOUNG MEN NEED ENCOURAGING BECAUSE OF THE SORROW IT WILL SAVE THEM

For another thing, young men need encouraging to begin serving God now, because of the sorrow it will save them. Sin is the mother of all sorrow. And no other sort of sin seems to give a man so much misery and pain as the sins of his youth. The foolish acts he did, the time he wasted, the mistakes he made, the bad company he kept, the harm he did himself (to both body and soul), the chances of happiness he threw away, the opportunities for usefulness he neglected—these are all things that often embitter the conscience of an old man. They throw a gloom on the evening of his days; they fill the closing hours of his life with self-reproach and shame.

Some men could tell you of the premature *loss of health* brought on by youthful sins. Disease racks their limbs with pain, and life is almost a weariness. Their muscle strength is so wasted that a grasshopper seems a burden. Their eyesight has become prematurely dim, and their natural strength has weakened. The sun of their health has gone down while it is still day and they mourn to see their flesh and body wasting away. Believe me, it is a bitter cup to drink.

Others could give you sad accounts of the *consequences of idleness*. They threw away the golden opportunity for learning. They would not get wisdom at a time when their minds were most able to receive it, and their memories most able to retain it. And now it is too late. They have not got the time to sit down and learn. They have no longer the same power, even if they did have the time. Lost time can never be redeemed. This too is a bitter cup to drink.

Others could tell you of grievous *mistakes in judgment*, from which they suffer for the rest of their lives. They wanted things their own way. They would not take advice. They formed some attachment which has been totally ruinous to their happiness. They chose a profession for which they were entirely unsuited. They see it all now... But their eyes are only opened when the mistake cannot be retrieved. This is indeed a bitter cup to drink.

Young men, young men, I wish you could truly know the comfort of a conscience which is not burdened with a long list of *youthful* sins. They are wounds that pierce the deepest. They are arrows that drink up a man's spirit. They are the poison that enters into the soul. Be merciful to yourselves. Seek the Lord early on in life and you will be spared many a bitter tear.

This is the truth that Job seems to have felt. He says, 'For you write bitter things against me and make me inherit the iniquities of my youth.'[31] Job's friend, Zophar, seems to have felt the same way, saying that the wicked person will discover that 'his bones

---

31   Job 13:26

are full of his youthful vigor, but it will lie down with him in the dust.'[32]

David seems to have felt it as well. He says to the Lord, 'Remember not the sins of my youth or my transgressions.'[33] Theodore Beza, the great Swiss Reformer, felt it so strongly that he included a special clause in his will; he noted that it was a special mercy that he had been called out from the world, by the grace of God, at the age of sixteen.

Go and ask an older Christian man for his opinion—I think many would say the same sort of thing. 'Oh, how I long that I could live my young days over again!' 'How I wish I had lived my early life better!' 'How I wish that I had not laid the foundation of bad habits so strongly in the springtime of my life!'

Young men, I want to save you from all this sorrow, if I can. Hell itself is truth which is known too late. Be wise before then. What youth sows, old age must reap. Do not give the most precious season of your life to things which will not comfort you in the latter part of your life. Instead, sow seeds of righteousness; clear your heart of weeds; and do not sow not among thorns.

Sin may come easily now, it may run smoothly off your tongue while you are young. But depend on it, you and sin will meet again before too long, whether you like it or not. Old wounds will often ache and give you pain long after they are healed, when only a scar remains; that is what you will find with your sins. The footprints of animals have been found on the surface of rocks

---

32   Job 20:11
33   Psalm 25:7

that were once wet sand, thousands of years after the animal that made them has perished and passed away; that is what you will find with your sins.

Benjamin Franklin is once supposed to have said: 'Experience keeps a dear school, but fools will learn in no other.' In other words, experience comes through costly mistakes, but fools will not learn in any other way. I want you all to escape the misery of learning in that school. I want you to avoid the wretchedness that youthful sins are sure to bring your way. This is another reason why I want to encourage and exhort you.

2. DANGERS TO YOUNG MEN

There are some particular dangers which young men need to be warned about. I am fully aware that *all* souls are in fearful peril. Whether we are young or old, it makes no difference. We all have a race to run, a battle to fight, a heart to subdue, a world to overcome, a body to control, a Devil to resist. We may well ask: who is up to such a task? But every age and stage has its own particular snares and temptations and it is good to know what they are. 'Forewarned is forearmed', the proverb says. If I can just persuade you to be on your guard against the dangers I list here, I am sure it will be of fundamental benefit to your soul.

PRIDE

One danger to young men is pride. Pride is the oldest sin in the world. Indeed, it existed before the world. Satan and his angels fell by pride. In Jude 6, we learn that they were not satisfied with their 'first estate'.[34] And, in this way, pride supplied hell with its first inhabitants.

Pride cast Adam out of paradise. Adam was not content with the place God had assigned him. He tried to raise himself up and he fell. And sin, sorrow and death entered the world by pride.

Pride naturally sits in all our hearts. We are born proud. Pride makes us self-satisfied, it makes us think we are good enough as we are, it closes our ears to advice, it refuses the gospel of Christ, and turns everyone to his own way. But pride never reigns anywhere so powerfully as it does in the heart of a young man.

How common it is to see young men who are self-confident, arrogant and unwilling to be advised! How often they can be rude and discourteous to those about them, thinking that they are not being valued and honoured as much as they deserve! How often young men fail to stop and listen to a hint from someone who is older! They think they know everything. How conceited they are when it comes to their own wisdom. They reckon older people (especially their relations) are rather stupid and slow. They think they need no teaching or instruction themselves; they think they understand everything. It makes them almost angry to be spoken to or challenged. Like young horses, they cannot bear the least bit of control. They must be independent and have things their own way. Rather like the men in the book of Job, they seem to think: 'No doubt (we) are the people, and wisdom will die with (us)!'[35] This is all pride.

---

34   Jude 6
35   Job 12:2

In 1 Kings 12, we read about Rehoboam who scorned the advice of the old, experienced men who stood before his father, and took the advice of the young men of his own generation. He lived to reap the consequences of his foolishness. There are many like him.

In Luke 15, we read the story of a younger son who demanded his share of his father's inheritance. He could not bring himself to live quietly under his father's roof, so he chose to go to a far-off country and be his own master. Like the little child that leaves its mother's side and walks all alone, the son soon regretted his foolishness. He became wiser when he had to eat the pigs' food. But there are many like him.

Young men, I beseech you earnestly, beware of pride. Two things are said to be very rare sights in the world: one is a young man who is humble, and the other is an old man who is content. I fear this is only too true.

Do be not proud of your own abilities, your own strength, your own knowledge, your own appearance or your own cleverness. Do not be not proud of yourself or anything that you have. It all comes from not knowing yourself and the world. The older you grow and the more you see, the less you will find reason for being proud. Ignorance and inexperience are the pedestal of pride. Once the pedestal is removed, pride will soon come down.

Remember how often the Bible reminds us about the value of a humble spirit. Paul warns us in the strongest terms 'not to think of ourselves more highly than we ought.'[36] How plainly we are told in 1 Corinthians that: 'If anyone imagines that he knows something, he does not yet know as he ought to know.'[37] How clear and strict the command in Colossians 3 is: 'put on, then … humility'[38] And again, in 1 Peter, 'clothe yourselves… with humility towards one another'.[39] I am afraid to say that, for many, this particular piece of clothing is nowhere to be seen in their spiritual wardrobe!

Think of the great example that our Lord Jesus Christ gives us in this respect. He washed the feet of his disciples, saying, 'I have given you an example, that you also should do just as I have done to you.'[40] Again, 'though he was rich, yet for your sake he became poor.'[41] And again, 'but emptied himself, by taking the form of a servant, being born in the likeness of men. And being found in human form, he humbled himself.'[42] There is no doubt that being proud is being like the devil and sinful Adam, rather than being like Christ. How can it possibly be contemptible or weak or to be like Christ?

Think of the wisest man that ever lived: I am thinking of King Solomon. He speaks of himself as a 'little child', as one who did 'not know how to go out or come in' or manage by himself.[43] His brother Absalom was completely different! He thought he was

---

36   Romans 12:3
37   1 Corinthians 8:2
38   Colossians 3:12
39   1 Peter 5:5
40   John 13:15
41   2 Corinthians 8:9
42   Philippians 2:7-8
43   1 Kings 3:7-8

equal to anything: 'Oh that I were judge in the land! Then every man with a dispute or cause might come to me, and I would give him justice.'[44] Or how about his brother Adonijah, who 'exalted himself, saying, "I will be king."'[45] Humility was the beginning of Solomon's wisdom, as he explains: 'Do you see a man who is wise in his own eyes? There is more hope for a fool than for him.'[46]

Young men, take these verses to heart. Do not be too confident in your own judgment. Stop being sure that you are always right, and that others are wrong. Be distrustful of your own opinion when you find it contradicts the opinion of those who are older than you, especially that of your own parents. Age gives experience and it therefore deserves respect. It is a mark of Elihu's wisdom (in the book of Job), that he 'had waited to speak to Job because they (Job's three friends) were older than he.'[47] And afterwards he said, 'I am young in years, and you are aged; therefore I was timid and afraid to declare my opinion to you.'[48] Modesty and silence are beautiful graces in young people. Never be ashamed of being a learner: Jesus was a learner when he was 12 years old – when he was found by his parents in the temple, he was 'sitting among the teachers, listening to them and asking them questions.'[49] The wisest men would tell you they are always learners, and that they are humbled to find how little they know after all. The great Sir Isaac Newton used to say that he felt he was no better than a little

---

44   2 Samuel 15:4
45   1 Kings 1:5
46   Proverbs 26:12
47   Job 32:4
48   Job 32:6-7
49   Luke 2:46

child who had picked up a few precious stones on the shore of the sea of knowledge.

Young men, if you want to be wise, if you want to be happy, remember this warning: *beware of pride*.

LOVE OF PLEASURE

Another danger to young men is the love of pleasure. Youth is the time when our passions are strongest: they are like unruly children, they cry loudly for indulgence. Youth is the time when we have generally most health and strength; death seems far away. Enjoying ourselves in this life seems everything. Youth is the time when we generally have fewest earthly worries or anxieties to take up our attention. And all these things help to make young men think of pleasure more than anything else. 'I serve lusts and pleasures.' For most young men, that is the real answer to the question: 'whose servant are you?'

Young men, I would run out of time if I were to try and tell you what fruits of this love of pleasure produces; all the ways in which it may do you harm. Why should I speak of making merry, feasting, gambling and the like? There are few men who do not know something of these things by bitter experience. And these are just a few examples. Everything that gives a feeling of excitement for the moment, everything that drowns thought and keeps the mind in a constant whirl, everything that indulges the senses and gratifies our sinful desires—these are the sort of things that have mighty power at your time of life. And they owe their power to the love of pleasure. Be on your guard. Do not be like those who Paul speaks of as, 'lovers of pleasure rather than lovers of God'.[50]

Remember what I say: If you devote yourself to earthly pleasures, these are the things that murder souls. There is no way that is more guaranteed to get a dulled conscience and a hard, impenitent heart than to give way to the desires of the flesh and mind. It seems nothing at first, but it has a devastating effect in the long run.

Consider what Peter says: 'I urge you… to abstain from the passions of the flesh, which wage war against your soul.'[51] They destroy the soul's peace, they break down its strength, they lead it into hard captivity, and they make it a slave.

Consider what Paul says: 'Put to death, therefore, what is earthly in you'.[52] 'Those who belong to Christ Jesus have crucified the flesh with its passions and desires.'[53] 'I discipline my body and keep it under control.'[54] Once, the body was a perfect home for the soul; now it is falling apart, it is corrupt and disordered, it needs constant watching. It is a burden to the soul, not an asset; a hindrance, not a help. The body may become a useful servant, but it is always a bad master.

Consider Paul's words again: 'put on the Lord Jesus Christ, and make no provision for the flesh, to gratify its desires.'[55] Robert

50   2 Timothy 3:4
51   1 Peter 2:11
52   Colossians 3:5
53   Galatians 5:24
54   1 Corinthians 9:27
55   Romans 13:14

Leighton (a seventeenth-century Archbishop of Glasgow) said of these verses: 'These are the words, the very reading of which so wrought with Augustine, that from a licentious young man he turned a faithful servant of Jesus Christ.' Augustine was miraculously converted as a young man from a life of debauchery to become wise and godly.[56] Young men, I wish this might be the case with all of you.

Remember, again, if you devote yourself to earthly pleasures, you will find that they are unsatisfying, empty and futile. In the vision in Revelation 9, there were locusts 'with crowns of gold' on their heads, but they also had stings in their tails.[57] Earthly pleasures are like that. Like the locusts, you will find that they have stings, real stings in their tails. 'All that glitters is not gold', as the saying goes. Not everything that tastes sweet turns out to be good. Not everything that pleases for a short time turns out to bring real, lasting pleasure.

Go and take your fill of earthly pleasures if you want to: your heart will never be truly satisfied by them. There will always be a voice within, crying, 'Give and give!'—like an insatiable leech.[58] There is an empty place within us which nothing but God can fill. You will find, as Solomon did from bitter experience, that earthly pleasures are but a mere shadow; they are meaningless, a chasing after the wind; they are 'whitewashed tombs, which outwardly appear beautiful, but within are full of dead people's bones and all

---

56   Augustine (354-430 AD) eventually became Bishop of Hippo in Northern Africa and a leader in the early Christian church.

57   Rev 9:3

58   Proverbs 30:15

uncleanness.'[59] Much better to be wise before it is too late. Much better to write 'poison' on all earthly pleasures. Even those that are permissible must be used with moderation. They are all soul-destroying, if you give them your heart. Thomas Adams, writing about 2 Peter, puts it like this: 'Pleasure must first have the warrant that it be without sin; then the measure, that it be without excess.' We must be certain that the pleasure does not involve sin; also, that it does not involve excess.

And here, I will not hold back from reminding all young men about the seventh commandment: 'You shall not commit adultery.'[60] We are commanded to avoid adultery, sexual immorality and impurity of every kind. I fear there is often a lack of plain speaking about this part of God's law. But when I see how the prophets and apostles dealt with this subject; when I observe the openness with which the great Protestant Reformers of our own church denounced it; when I read in the Bible about the adulterous Reuben (Jacob's son), Hophni and Phinehas (the sons of Eli), and Amnon (son of David); when I see how many young men walk in their footsteps, I cannot, with a good conscience, hold my peace. I doubt whether the world is any better off for the excessive silence which surrounds this commandment. For myself, I feel that I would be being prudish, unbiblical and over-sensitive if failed to speak to young men frankly about this issue. It is, after all, chiefly 'a young man's sin.'

---

59   Ps 39:6, Eccl 1:14, Matt 23:27
60   Exodus 20:14

The breaking of the seventh commandment is the sin which 'take(s) away the understanding', as Hosea says.[61] It is the sin that leaves deeper scars upon the soul than any other sin that a man can commit. It is a sin that causes the death of thousands in every age, a sin that has overthrown a many a believer in time past. Samson and David are fearful proofs.[62] It is the sin that man dares to smile at, and glosses over calling it jollity, inconsistency, wildness or unpredictability. But it is the sin that the devil particularly rejoices over, for he is the 'unclean spirit'.[63] It is a sin that God particularly hates: he 'will judge the sexually immoral and adulterous.'[64]

Young men, if you love life, then 'flee from sexual immorality.'[65] Run away from it! 'Let no one deceive you with empty words, for because of these things the wrath of God comes upon the sons of disobedience.'[66] Run away from any *opportunity* for it, run from the company or friendship of those who might draw you into it, run from the places where you might be tempted to it. Read what our Lord says: 'But I say to you that everyone who looks at a woman with lustful intent has already committed adultery with her in his heart.'[67] Be godly like Job who made this resolution: 'I have made a covenant with my eyes; how then could I gaze at a virgin?.'[68] Run away from any *talk* of it. It is one of those

---

61   Hosea 4:11
62   Judges 16:1, 2 Sam 11:4
63   eg Luke 4:33, Rev 16:13
64   Hebrews 13:4
65   1 Corinthians 6:18
66   Ephesians 5:6
67   Matthew 5:28
68   Job 31:1

things that should never be the subject of idle chat. You cannot handle tar and avoid being dirtied by that black, sticky mess. Run away from any *thought* of it—resist day-dreams and fantasies, put them to death, pray against them. Make any sacrifice you need to, rather than giving into them. Imagination is the hotbed where this sin is too often hatched. Guard your thoughts, and there will be little danger about your deeds.

Think clearly about this warning I am giving you. If you forget everything else, do not forget this.

FAILURE TO THINK

Another danger to young men is failure to think. It is one simple reason why thousands of souls are lost forever. Men will not think clearly, they will not look forward, they will not look around them, they will not reflect on the end of their lives and the inevitable consequences of their current ways. They will awake at last to find they are damned for a failure to think.

Young men, no-one is in more danger of this than you. You know very little of the dangers around you and so you are careless about how you walk. You hate the bother of sober, quiet thinking and so you make wrong decisions and end up in trouble. The young man Esau was desperate for his brother's food and, therefore, he sold his inheritance. He never stopped to think how much he would want it in the future.[69] The young men, Simeon and Levi, were desperate to avenge their sister Dinah when she was raped and they killed the men of Shechem. They never

---

69   Gen 25:29-34

stopped to think how much trouble and anxiety they might bring on their father Jacob and his family.[70] Job seems to have been especially concerned about this lack of thought among his children: after they had been feasting: 'And when the days of the feast had run their course, Job would send and consecrate them, and he would rise early in the morning and offer burnt offerings according to the number of them all. For Job said, "It may be that my children have sinned, and cursed God in their hearts." Thus Job did continually.'[71]

Believe me, this world is not a world in which we can do well without thinking. That is especially true in the matter of our souls. 'Don't think about it,' whispers Satan. He knows that an unconverted heart is like the accounts of a dishonest trader: they do not bear close inspection. 'Consider your ways,' says the word of God—stop and think, weigh things up thoroughly, be wise.[72] The Spanish proverb is true: 'Hurry comes from the devil.' It is said that men marry in haste and then repent at leisure. In the same way, they make mistakes about their souls in a minute, and then suffer for it for years. A careless employee might do something wrong and then say, 'I didn't even think about it.' In the same way, young men run into sin and then say, 'I didn't think about it; it did not look like sin.' Not look like sin! How would you like things to be? Sin will not come to you saying, 'I am sin.' It would do you very little harm if it did. Sin always seems 'good', 'pleasing to the eye', and 'desirable' at the time.[73] Get wisdom!

---

70   Gen 34
71   Job 1:5
72   Haggai 1:5
73   Gen 3:6

Get good judgment! Remember the words of Solomon: 'Ponder the path of your feet; then all your ways will be sure..'[74] It is a wise saying of Lord Bacon, 'Do nothing rashly. Stay a little, that you make an end the sooner.'

Some, I dare say, will say that I am being unreasonable, that youth is not the time of life when people ought to be serious and thoughtful. I would answer that there is very little danger of being *too* serious and thoughtful. Foolish talking, jesting, joking and excessive merriment are only too common. There may be a time for all these things; but to be lightweight and trivial *all the time* is anything but wise. What does one of the wisest of men of all say about it?[75]

> *It is better to go to the house of mourning than to go to the house of feasting, for this is the end of all mankind, and the living will lay it to heart. Sorrow is better than laughter, for by sadness of face the heart is made glad. The heart of the wise is in the house of mourning, but the heart of fools is in the house of mirth.*

Bible commentator Matthew Henry tells the story of a great statesman, Sir Francis Walsingham who was Queen Elizabeth I's Secretary of State in charge of intelligence. In his old age, he retired from public life and gave himself to serious thought. Some of his former friends came to visit and told him he was becoming melancholy.

---

74   Proverbs 4:26
75   Ecclesiastes 7:2-4

'No,' he replied, *'I am serious; for all are serious round
about me. God is serious in observing us; Christ is serious
in interceding for us; the Spirit is serious in striving with
us; the truths of God are serious; our spiritual enemies are
serious in their endeavours to ruin us; poor lost sinners
are serious in hell; and why then should not you and I be
serious too?'*

Young men, do learn to think! Learn to think carefully about
what you are doing and where you are going. Make time for calm
reflection. Search your hearts and be still.[76] Remember my warning: Do not be lost simply for failure to think.

CONTEMPT OF REAL FAITH

Another danger to young men is contempt of genuine faith. It
is another of your special dangers. I always observe that no-one
pays so little outward respect to true faith as young men. No-one
is more careless about the 'means of grace' than young men.[77] It
tends to be the young men who fail to take part in our church
services, use their Bibles and prayer books so little, who sing so
little, who listen to preaching so little. They are the ones who are
generally absent from prayer meetings, Bible studies and other
midweek helps to the soul. Young men seem to think they do not
need these things; they may be good for women and old men, but
not for them. They seem to be ashamed of seeming to care about

---

76   Ps 4:4
77   'Means of grace' are the ways in which God works to communicate to
the hearts of men and women in church services, through bible reading, prayer,
and especially preaching.

their souls. You might even think that they thought it would be a disgrace to go to heaven at all. And this is being contemptuous of real faith! It is the same kind of attitude which led the young people of Bethel to mock Elisha in 2 Kings – they 'jeered at him, saying, "Go up, you baldhead!"'[78] And of this attitude, I say to all young men: beware! If it is worthwhile to have a faith, it is worthwhile to be in earnest about it.

Contempt of holy things is the quickest road to backsliding and falling away. Once a man begins to jest and jokes about any part of Christianity, I am never surprised to hear that he has turned out to be a complete unbeliever.

Young men, have you really made up your minds about this? Have you looked squarely into the gulf which is in front of you if you persist in despising real faith? Remember what David says: 'The fool says in his heart, "There is no God."'[79] The fool, and no-one but the fool! The fool says there is no God—but, of course, he has never managed to prove it! Remember, if there was ever a book, which has been proved true from beginning to end, by every kind of evidence, that book is the Bible. It has withstood the attacks of all its enemies and faultfinders. 'The word of the Lord's proves true.'[80] It has been tested in every way, and the more it has been tested, the more clearly it has been shown to be the very handiwork of God himself. What will you believe if you do not believe the Bible? There is no choice but to believe something ridiculous and absurd. Depend on it, no man is so ridiculously

---

78   2 Kings 2:23
79   Psalm 14:1
80   Psalm 18:30

credulous as the man who denies that the Bible is the word of God. And if it is the word of God, take care that you do not despise it.

People will often say that there are difficulties and inconsistencies in the Bible, things that are hard to understood. It would not be God's book if there were not! And what if there are? You do not despise medicines because you cannot explain everything that is achieved by them. But whatever people may say, the things that are necessary to salvation are as clear as daylight. Be very sure of this: people never reject the Bible because they cannot understand it. They understand it only too well; they understand that it condemns their own behaviour; they understand that it speaks out against their own sins and summons them to judgment. They try to believe it is false and useless, because they do not want to admit that it is true. 'A bad life,' said the famous Lord Rochester, laying his hand on the Bible, 'a bad life is the only grand objection to this book.'[81] 'Men question the truth of Christianity,' said Anglican clergyman Robert South, 'because they hate the practice of it.'

Young men, when did God ever fail to keep his word? Never. He has always done what he said he would do; when he speaks, his word is totally effective. Did he fail to keep his word at the flood? No. Did he fail with Sodom and Gomorrah? No. Did he fail with unbelieving Jerusalem? No. He has never failed to fulfil his word. Take care, in case you are found among those who despise God's word.

---

81   John Wilmot, 2nd Earl of Rochester (1647-80), was an adviser to King Charles II and a member of his court.

Never laugh at religion. Never make a joke about sacred things. Never mock those who are serious and in earnest about their souls. The time may come when you will consider the ones you laughed at to be happy; a time when your laughter will be turned into sorrow, and your mockery into heaviness.

FEAR OF OTHERS' OPINION

Another danger to young men is the fear of man's opinion. 'Fear of man' will indeed prove to be a snare.[82] It is terrible to observe the power which it has over most minds, and especially over the minds of the young. Few young people seem to have opinions of their own, or to think for themselves. Like dead fish, they go with the stream and the tide; what others think right, they think right; what others call wrong, they call wrong too. There are few original thinkers in the world. Most people are like sheep: they follow a leader. If it was the fashion of the day to be Catholic, they would be Catholic; if it was fashionable to be Muslim, they would be Muslim. They dread the idea of going against the tide. In a word, the opinion of the day becomes their religion, their creed, their Bible, and their God.

The thought 'What will my friends say or think of me?' nips many a good inclination in the bud. The fear of being observed, laughed at or ridiculed prevents many a good habit being taken up. There are Bibles that would be read this very day if the owners dared to do so. They know they ought to read them, but they are afraid: 'What will people say?' There are knees that would be bent

---

82 Proverbs 29:25

in prayer this very evening, but the fear of man forbids it: 'What would my wife, my brother, my friend, my companion say if they saw me praying?' This is such wretched slavery! But I fear it is very common. 'I feared the people and obeyed their voice,' said Saul to Samuel, and he broke God's commandment.[83] 'I was afraid of the Jews,' said Zedekiah, the graceless king of Judah—and he disobeyed the advice which Jeremiah gave him.[84] Herod was afraid of what his guests would think of him, so he did something that made him exceedingly sorry and 'distressed': he beheaded John the Baptist.[85] Pilate feared offending the Jews, so he did something which he knew in his conscience was unjust: he handed Jesus over to be crucified.[86] If this is not slavery, what is?

Young men, I want you all to be free from this captivity. I want each of you not to care about the opinion of other people, when the right path is clear to you. Believe me, it is a great thing to be able to say 'No!' This was good King Jehoshaphat's weak point: he was too easy and pliable in his dealings with King Ahab, and that led to many of his troubles.[87] Learn to say, 'No!' Do not let the fear of not seeming good-natured make you unable to do that. When sinners tempt and entice you, you must be able to say decisively that you will not consent.[88]

---

83   1 Samuel 15:24
84   Jer 38:19
85   Matt 14:9
86   Mk 15:15
87   1 Ki 22:4
88   Proverbs 1:10

Think about how *unreasonable* this 'fear of man' is. Another person's enmity is so short-lived; they can do so little harm to you! Consider Isaiah's words:[89]

> *'who are you that you are afraid of man who dies, of the son of man who is made like grass, and have forgotten the Lord, your Maker, who stretched out the heavens and laid the foundations of the earth?'*

And how *useless* this fear is! No-one will really think any the better of you because of it. The world respects those most who act boldly for God. 'Let us burst their bonds apart and cast away their cords from us', as the Psalmist says.90 Never be ashamed of letting people see that you want to go to heaven. Do not think of it as a disgrace to show yourself to be a servant of God. Never be afraid of doing what is right.

Remember the words of the Lord Jesus: 'do not fear those who kill the body but cannot kill the soul. Rather fear him who can destroy both soul and body in hell.'[91] Only try to please God – and he can soon make others pleased with you. 'When a man's ways please the Lord, he makes even his enemies to be at peace with him.'[92]

Young men, be courageous. Do not care about what the world says or thinks: you will not always be with the world. Can other people save your soul? No. Will other people be your judge in the

---

89   Isaiah 51:12-13

90   Psalm 2:3

91   Matthew 10:28

92   Proverbs 16:7

great and dreadful day of account? No. Can other people give you a good conscience in life, a good hope in death, a good answer on the day of resurrection? No! No! No! Other people can do nothing of the sort. Then 'fear not the reproach of man, nor be dismayed at their revilings. For the moth will eat them up like a garment, and the worm will eat them like wool.'[93] Call to mind the saying of good Colonel James Gardiner: 'I fear God, and therefore I have none else to fear.'[94] Go and be like him.

These are the warnings I give you. Take them to heart. They are worth thinking over. Unless I am much mistaken, they are greatly needed. I pray that they have not been offered to you in vain.

---

93   Isaiah 51:7-8
94   Col James Gardiner (1687-1745) was a godly preacher who was marvellously converted by reading Thomas Watson's book, *Heaven Taken by Storm*.

3. GENERAL ADVICE
TO YOUNG MEN

Thirdly, I wish to give some general advice to young men.

AIM TO GET A CLEAR VIEW
ABOUT THE EVIL OF SIN

Young men, if you truly knew what sin is and what sin has done, you would not think it strange that I exhort you as I do. You do not see it in its true colours. Your eyes are naturally blind to its guilt and danger, and so you cannot understand what makes me so anxious for you. Do not let the devil succeed in persuading you that sin is a small matter!

Think for a moment *what the Bible says about sin*:

- how it dwells naturally in the heart of every man and woman alive[95]

Eccl 7:20; Rom 3:23

- how it defiles our thoughts, words and actions – and does so continually[96]

- how it renders us all guilty and abominable in the sight of a holy God[97]

- how it leaves us utterly without hope of salvation, if we rely on ourselves[98]

- how its fruit in this world is shame; and its wages in the world to come are death[99]

Think calmly and clearly about all this. I ask you, which is worse: to be dying of cancer and not to know it; or be a living man, dying of sin and not know about it?

Think about what an *awful change sin has worked* on our nature. We are no longer what we were when God formed man and woman out of the dust of the ground. Adam was created by God's hand as upright and sinless.[100] On the day of his creation he was, like everything else, 'very good'.[101] But what are we now?

- fallen creatures, ruins, beings that bear the marks of corruption everywhere

- our hearts are like Nebuchadnezzar's, degraded and earthly, looking down at everything on earth and not up

---

96   Gen 6:5; Matt 15:19
97   Isa 64:6; Hab 1:13
98   Ps 143:2; Rom 3:20
99   Rom 6:21,23
100   Ecclesiastes 7:29
101   Genesis 1:31

to heaven[102]

- our longings and desires are like a house in complete disarray, subject to our whims, all extravagance and confusion

- our understanding is like a faulty, flickering lamp, powerless to guide us, not knowing good from evil

- our will is like a rudderless ship, tossed to and fro by every desire; the only constant is choosing any way rather than God's

What wrecks we are, compared with what we might have been! It is no surprise that the Bible uses images of blindness, deafness, disease, sleep and death when the Spirit describes the state of men and women. And remember, we are like this because we were made so by sin.

Think too *what it has cost to pay the debt* that is owed because of sin, the cost of reconciliation, the cost of providing pardon and forgiveness for sinners. God's own Son had to come into the world and take the nature of a man, in order to pay the price of our redemption and deliver us from the curse of a broken law. He who was with the Father in the beginning, and by whom all things were made, had to suffer for sin, the just for the unjust. He had to die the death of a criminal before the way to heaven could be laid open to any soul. Think about how the Lord Jesus Christ was despised and rejected by men, scourged and beaten, mocked and insulted. Think about how he bled on the cross of Calvary; hear

---

102   Daniel 4:30

him crying in agony, 'My God, my God, why have you forsaken me?'[103] Remember how the sun stopped shining, and the rocks split.[104] Then understand, young men, the evil and guilt of sin.

Think, also, what *sin has already done* on earth. Think how it forced Adam and Eve out of the Garden of Eden, how it brought the flood upon the old world, how it caused fire to come down on Sodom and Gomorrah, how it drowned Pharaoh and his armies in the Red Sea, how it destroyed the seven wicked nations of Canaan, how it scattered the 12 tribes of Israel over the face of the globe. Sin alone did all this.

Think, moreover, of all the *misery and sorrow that sin has caused* and continues to cause today. Pain, disease and death; conflict, quarrels, and divisions; envy, jealousy and bitterness; deceit, fraud and cheating; violence, oppression and robbery; selfishness, unkindness and ingratitude. All these are the fruits of sin. Sin is the parent of them all. It is sin that has so marred and spoiled the face of God's creation.

Young men, if you think carefully about this, you will not be surprised that we preach as we do. Surely, if you were to think it through properly, you would reject sin forever. Will you play with poison? Will you trifle with hell? Will you play with fire? Will you shelter your deadliest enemy in your heart? Will you go on living as if it did not matter whether your own sins were forgiven or not; as if it made no difference whether sin had control over you, or whether you had control over sin? Please wake up! Please

---

103   Matthew 27:46
104   Luke 23:45; Matthew 27:51

get a sense of sin's sinfulness and danger! Remember the words of Solomon: 'Fools'—only fools—'mock at sin.'[105]

Please hear my request! I pray that God would teach you the real evil of sin. If you want your soul to be saved, get up and pray.

AIM TO GET TO KNOW OUR LORD JESUS CHRIST

This is, of course, the most important thing about faith. This is the cornerstone of Christianity. Until you know this, my warnings and advice will be utterly useless – and all your efforts, whatever they may be, will be pointless. A pocket watch without a mainspring[106] is totally useless, just like religion without Christ.

But let me not be misunderstood. It is not simply knowing Christ's name that I am talking about. It is knowing his mercy, grace and power; knowing him not by what you hear but by the experience of your heart. I want you to know him by faith; I want you, as Paul puts it, to know 'the power of his resurrection ... becoming like him in his death.'[107] I want you to be able to say of him, he is my peace and my strength, my life and my comfort, my great physician and my shepherd, my Saviour and my God.

Why do I make such a point of this? I do so because it is in Christ alone that 'all fullness of God was pleased to dwell.'[108] Be-

---

105   Proverbs 14:9
106   Or a digital watch without a battery.
107   Philippians 3:10
108   Colossians 1:19

cause it is Christ alone who supplies all our needs.[109] By ourselves, we are all poor, empty creatures – empty of righteousness and peace, empty of strength and comfort, empty of courage and patience, empty of power to stand or go on, empty of power to make progress in this evil world. It is in Christ alone that all these things are to be found: grace, peace, wisdom, righteousness, sanctification and redemption. The amount we rely upon him determines our strength as Christians. It is only when confidence in self is nothing and confidence in Christ is everything—it is only then that we can do great things. It is only then that we are armed for the battle of life, and can be victorious. It is only then that we are prepared for the journey of life, and can go forward. To rely on Christ, to draw everything from Christ, to do all things in the strength of Christ, to be always looking to Christ, this is the true secret of spiritual prosperity. 'I can do all this,' says Paul, 'through him who strengthens me.'[110]

Young men, I set before you today Jesus Christ as the guardian of your souls. I invite you to begin by going to him if this is what you really want. Let this be your first step: *go to Christ*. Do you want to consult a friend? He is the best friend: 'a friend that sticks closer than a brother.'[111]

Do you feel unworthy because of your sins? Do not be afraid: his blood cleanses from all sin. He says, 'though your sins are like

---

109   Philippians 4:19
110   Philippians 4:13
111   Proverbs 18:24

scarlet, they shall be as white as snow; though they are red like crimson, they shall become like wool.'[112]

Do you feel weak, and unable to follow him? Do not be afraid: he will give you power to become sons of God. He will give you the Holy Spirit to dwell in you, and mark you for his own; he will give you a new heart, he will put a new spirit in you.

Are you troubled or plagued by particular failings? Do not be afraid: there is no evil spirit that Jesus cannot cast out; there is no disease of the soul that he cannot heal.

Do you feel doubts and fears? Cast them on to him: 'come to me,' he says; 'whoever comes to me I will never cast out.'[113] He totally understands the heart of a young man. He knows your trials and your temptations, your difficulties and your enemies. In his days on earth, he was like you: he was a young man at Nazareth. He has experienced the mind of a young man. He is moved by feeling your troubles, for he suffered himself when he was tempted; and he has been tempted in every way, just as we are.[114] You can have no excuse if you turn away from such a Saviour and friend as this.

Hear my appeal to you: if you love life, aim to get to know Jesus Christ.

---

112   Isaiah 1:18
113   John 6:37
114   Heb 2:18, 4:15

DO NOT FORGET THAT NOTHING IS AS IMPORTANT AS YOUR SOUL

Your soul is eternal. It will live forever. The world and everything in it will pass away. As firm, solid, beautiful and well-ordered as it is, the world will come to an end. 'The earth and the works that are done on it will be exposed.'[115] The works of politicians, writers, painters and architects are all short-lived; your soul will outlive them all. One day, the angel's voice will proclaim: 'There will be no more delay!'[116] But that will never be said of your souls.

I beg you to try and understand the fact that your soul is the one thing worth living for. It is the part of you which ought always to be considered first. No place, no job is good for you if it injures your soul. No friend, no companion deserves your confidence if they make light of the importance of your soul. Anyone who hurts your body, your property or your character harms you only temporarily. But the one who damages your soul is a true enemy.

Think for a moment why you were sent into the world. Not merely to eat and drink and satisfy your bodily desires; not merely to adorn your body, and follow its lusts wherever they might lead you; not merely to work and sleep and laugh and talk, and enjoy yourself and think of nothing beyond today. No! You are meant for something higher and better than this. You were placed here to train for eternity. Your body is meant to be a home for your immortal spirit. The body is meant to serve the soul. It is flying

---

115   2 Peter 3:10
116   Revelation 10:6

in the face of God's purposes when the soul serves the body. The Westminster Larger Catechism begins with this excellent question and answer: 'What is the chief and highest end of man?' 'To glorify God, and fully to enjoy him forever.'[117]

Young men, God shows no favouritism. He pays no attention to a man's looks, wallet, rank or job. He does not see things with man's eyes. The poorest believer that ever died in a workhouse is more noble in his sight than the richest sinner that ever died in a palace. God does not look at riches, titles, education, beauty or anything of the kind. God only looks at one thing, and that is the immortal soul. He measures all men by one standard, one measure, one test, one criterion, and that is *the state of their souls*.

Do not forget this. Keep the interests of your soul in mind, morning, noon and night. Get up each day desiring that your soul may prosper; lie down each evening asking yourself whether it has progressed. Remember Zeuxis, the great Greek painter of old.[118] When men asked him why he laboured so intensely, and took such extreme care with every picture, his simple answer was, 'I paint for eternity.' Do not be ashamed to be like him. Set your immortal soul before your mind's eye, and when people ask you why you live as you do, answer them in a similar spirit, 'I live for my soul.' Believe me, the day is fast approaching when the soul will be the one thing that men think of, and the only question of importance will be this, *'Is my soul lost or saved?'*

---

117   The Westminster Larger Catechism (1648) is a summary of Christian doctrine in the form of questions and answers.

118   Zeuxis (464-396 BC) was a painter during the golden age of Greece.

REMEMBER IT IS POSSIBLE TO BE BOTH
A YOUNG MAN AND A SERVANT OF GOD

It is possible to be a young man and serve God at the same time. I fear the snares and traps that Satan lays for you on this point. I fear lest he succeeds in filling your minds with the foolish notion that being a true Christian as a young man is impossible. I have seen many carried away by this delusion. I have heard it said, 'You are requiring the impossible in expecting so much faith from young people. Youth is no time for seriousness. Our desires are strong. It was never intended that we should control them, as you wish us to do. God meant us to enjoy ourselves. There will be time enough for religion in days to come.' And the world is only too ready to encourage this kind of talk. The world is only too ready to wink at youthful sins. The world appears to think it is totally normal that young men must 'sow their wild oats.' The world seems to take it for granted that young people must be irreligious, and that it is not possible for them to follow Christ.

Young men, I will ask you this simple question: Where will you find anything about this in the word of God? Where is the chapter or verse in the Bible which supports this kind of talk and the world's understanding? Doesn't the Bible speak to old and young alike without distinction? Isn't sin still sin, whether it is committed at the age of twenty or fifty? Will it count as even the slightest excuse on the day of judgment to say, 'I know I sinned, but I was young then'? Show some common sense, I beg you, by giving up such foolish excuses. You are responsible and accountable to God from the very moment that you know right and wrong.

I realise that young men face many difficulties; I do understand that. But it is *always* difficult to do the right thing. The path to heaven is always narrow, whether we are young or old. There are always difficulties, but God will give you grace to overcome them. God is not a hard task-master. He will not, like Pharaoh, require you to make bricks without straw.[119] He will take care that the path of plain duty is never impossible. He never laid commands on us which he would not give us power to perform.[120]

There are difficulties, certainly – but many a young man has overcome them before now, and so may you. Moses was a young man of passions like you, but see what is said of him in the Bible:

> *By faith Moses, when he was grown up, refused to be called the son of Pharaoh's daughter, choosing rather to be mistreated with the people of God than to enjoy the fleeting pleasures of sin. He considered the reproach of Christ greater wealth than the treasures of Egypt, for he was looking to the reward.[121]*

Daniel was a young man when he began to serve God in Babylon. He was surrounded by temptations of every kind. He had few friends on his side, and many against him. Yet Daniel's life was so blameless and consistent, that even his enemies could find no fault in him, 'unless we find it in connection with the law of his God'.[122] And these are not solitary cases. There is a cloud of witnesses whom I could name. Time would fail me if I were to tell

119   Ex 5:16
120   1 Cor 10:13
121   Hebrews 11:24-26
122   Daniel 6:5

you all about young Isaac[123], young Joseph[124], young Joshua[125], young Samuel[126], young David[127], young Solomon[128], young Abijah[129], young Obadiah[130], young Josiah[131], and young Timothy[132]. They were not angels, but men with hearts naturally like your own. They too had obstacles to contend with, lusts to put to death, trials to endure, hard roles to fill, like any of you. But young as they were, they all found it possible to serve God. Will they not all rise in judgment and declare you guilty if you persist in saying it cannot be done?

Young men, *try* to serve God. Resist the devil when he whispers that it is impossible. Try, and the Lord God of the promises will give you strength as you do so. He loves to meet those who strive to come to him, and he will meet you and give you the power that you feel you need. Be like the man in John Bunyan's *Pilgrim's Progress* who yearns to be allowed into the palace; be like him, go forward boldly and say: 'Set down my name.'[133] Our Lord says to us, 'Ask, and it will be given to you; seek, and you will

---

123   Genesis 22
124   Genesis 39
125   Exodus 17:9-14
126   1 Samuel 2:18-3:21
127   1 Samuel 16-17
128   1 Kings 3:4-9
129   2 Chronicles 13
130   1 Kings 18:3
131   2 Chronicles 34-35
132   Acts 16:1-3
133   John Bunyan's *Pilgrim's Progress* (1678) is an allegory of the Christian life, going from the heavy burden of sin, to conversion, to sanctification, to death and glorification. The metaphors in this paragraph (mountains, giants, lions) are scenes from the book.

find; knock, and it will be opened to you.'[134] His words are true, though I often hear them repeated mindlessly and indifferently. Difficulties which seem like mountains will melt away like snow in spring. Obstacles which seem like giants in the distant mist will dwindle into nothing when you face them head on. The lion in the way which you fear will prove to be chained up. If we believed the promises more, we would never be afraid of the obedience we owe. But remember that little encouragement I urge on you, and when Satan says to you, 'You cannot be a Christian while you are young,' answer him, 'Get behind me, Satan; with God's help, *I will try.*'

AIM TO MAKE THE BIBLE YOUR GUIDE AND ADVISER

For another thing, resolve to make the Bible your guide and adviser as long as you live. The Bible is God's merciful provision for sinful souls, the map by which we must steer our course if we want to gain eternal life. All we need to know to be peaceful, holy or happy, is richly contained in it. If a young man wants to know how to begin life well, let him hear what David says: 'How can a young man keep his way pure? By guarding it according to your word.'[135]

Young men, I challenge you to make a habit of reading the Bible, and not to let the habit be broken. Do not let the laughter of friends, nor the bad habits of the family you may live in—do

---

134   Matthew 7:7
135   Psalm 119:9

not let any of these things prevent you doing it. Decide that you will not only *have* a Bible, but also make time to *read* it too. Do not let anyone persuade you that it is only a book for Sunday school children and old women. It is the book from which King David got wisdom and understanding. It is the book which young Timothy knew from his childhood. Never be ashamed of reading it. Do not scorn the word.[136]

Read it *with prayer* for the Holy Spirit's grace to make you understand it. Bishop William Beveridge puts it well, 'A man may as soon read the letter of Scripture without eyes, as understand the spirit of it without grace.'[137]

Read it *reverently*, as the word of God, not as a human word.[138] Read it, believing implicitly that what it approves is right, and what it condemns is wrong. Be very sure that every doctrine which will not stand the test of Scripture is false. This will keep you from being tossed to and fro, and carried about by the dangerous 'popular opinion.' Be very sure that every *practice* in your life which is contrary to Scripture is sinful, and must be given up. This will settle many a question of conscience, and sort out many a doubt. Remember how differently two kings of Judah read the word of God: King Jehoiakim read it, and at once cut the writing to pieces, and burned it on the fire.[139] Why? Because his heart rebelled against it, and he was determined not to obey. King Josiah read

---

136   Proverbs 13:13
137   William Beveridge (1637-1708) was the Anglican Bishop of Asaph, England.
138   1 Thessalonians 2:13
139   Jeremiah 36:23

it, and at once tore his clothes, and cried mightily to the Lord.[140] And why? Because his heart was tender and obedient. He was ready to do anything which Scripture showed him was his duty. I long that you may follow the last of these two, and not the first!

And read it *regularly*. This is the only way to be 'competent in the Scriptures'.[141] A hasty glance at the Bible now and then does little good. At that rate, you will never become familiar with its treasures, or feel the sword of the Spirit fitted to your hand in the hour of conflict. But get your mind stocked with Scripture, by diligent reading, and you will soon discover its value and power. Texts will rise up in your hearts in the moment of temptation. Commands will suggest themselves in seasons of doubt. Promises will permeate your thoughts in the time of discouragement. And, in this way, you will experience the truth of David's words, 'I have stored up your word in my heart, that I might not sin against you.'[142] And the truth of Solomon's words too, 'When you walk, they will lead you; when you lie down, they will watch over you; and when you awake, they will talk with you.'[143]

I dwell on these things more because this is an age of reading. As it says in Ecclesiastes, 'Of making many books there is no end'.[144] Few of them, however, are really profitable. There is a fashion for cheap printing and publishing. Newspapers of ev-

---

140   2 Chronicles 34:19
141   Acts 18:24
142   Psalm 119:11
143   Proverbs 6:22
144   Ecclesiastes 12:12

ery sort abound, and the tone of some which have the widest circulation speaks badly of our society's tastes. Amidst the flood of dangerous reading, I plead for my Master's book. I call upon you not to forget the book of the soul. Do not let newspapers, novels and romances be read, while the prophets and apostles lie scorned. Do not let the exciting and licentious material swallow up your attention, while the edifying and the sanctifying can find no place in your mind.

Young men, give the Bible the honour it is due every day you live. Whatever you read, read that first. And beware of bad books: there are plenty of them. Take heed to what you read. I suspect there is more harm done to souls in this way than most people realise is possible. Value all books in proportion to how they agree with Scripture. Those that are nearest to it are the best, and those that are furthest from it and most contrary to it, are the worst.

NEVER MAKE AN INTIMATE FRIEND OF ANYONE WHO IS NOT A FRIEND OF GOD

Understand me rightly, I am not speaking of *acquaintances*. I do not mean that you ought to have nothing to do with anyone but true Christians. To take that line is neither possible nor desirable in this world. Christianity requires no-one to be discourteous.

But I do advise you to be very careful in your choice of *friends*. Do not open your heart to someone merely because they are clever, agreeable, good-natured, high-spirited and kind. These things are all very well in their way, but they are not everything. Never be satisfied with the friendship of anyone who will not be useful to your soul.

Believe me, the importance of this advice cannot be overrated. There is no telling the harm that is done by associating with godless companions and friends. The devil has few better strategies when it comes to ruining a man's soul. Grant him leeway in this, and he cares little about all the armour with which you may be armed against him. Good education, early habits of morality, sermons, books, stable homes, the influence of parents—the devil knows they will all be of little help if you cling to ungodly friends. You may resist many open temptations and refuse many plain snares. But once you take up with a bad companion, the devil is content. That awful chapter which describes Amnon's wicked behaviour towards Tamar, has these words right near the beginning of the account: 'But Amnon had a friend … a very crafty man.'[145] You must remember, we are all creatures of imitation: rules may teach us, but it is example that draws us. There is that characteristic in us all: we are always disposed to copy the ways of those with whom we live; and the more we like them, the stronger the disposition grows. Without our being aware of it, they influence our tastes and opinions. We gradually give up what they dislike and take up what they like, in order to become closer friends with them. And worst of all, we copy their ways in things that are *wrong* far more quickly than in things that are *right*. Health, unhappily, is not contagious; but disease is. It is far easier to catch a cold than to impart a glow; far easier to make each other's faith dwindle away, than grow and prosper.

---

145   2 Samuel 13:3

Young men, I ask you to take these things to heart. Before you let anyone become your constant companion, before you get into the habit of telling them everything, and going to them with all your troubles and all your pleasures—*before* you do this, just think about what I have been saying. Ask yourself, 'Will this be a useful friendship to me or not?'

'Bad company' does indeed 'ruin good morals.'[146] I wish that verse was written in hearts as often as it is in books. Good friends are among our greatest blessings. They may keep us back from much evil, encourage us on our journey, speak a timely word, draw us upward, and draw us on. But a bad friend is a positive misfortune, a weight continually dragging us down, and chaining us to earth. If you keep company with an irreligious man, it is more than probable that you will become like him in the end. That is the general outcome of all such friendships. The good go down to the bad; and the bad do not come up to the good. Even a stone will hollow out and erode when it is subject to a constant dripping of water. The world's proverb is only too correct: 'Clothes and company tell true tales about character.' 'Show me who a man lives with, and I will show you what he is,' say the Spaniards.

I dwell particularly upon this point because it has more to do with your prospects in life than it appears at first sight. If you ever marry, it is quite likely that you will choose a wife from among the friends of your friends. If Jehoshaphat's son Jehoram had not formed a friendship with Ahab's family, he would probably not

---

146   1 Corinthians 15:33

have married Ahab's daughter.[147] And who can calculate the importance of a right choice in marriage? It is a step which, according to the old saying, 'either makes a man or mars him.' The happiness of both of your lives will depend on it. Your wife will either help your soul or harm it: there is no happy medium. She will either fan the flame of faith in your heart, or throw cold water on it and make it burn low. She will either be wings or chains, either a spur or a rein to your Christianity, according to her character. He who finds a good wife certainly 'finds a good thing'.[148] But if you have the least wish to find one, be very careful how you choose your friends.

Do you ask me what kind of friends you shall choose? Choose friends who will benefit your soul, friends whom you can really respect, friends whom you would like to have near you on your deathbed, friends who live the Bible and are not afraid to speak to you about it, friends that you will not be ashamed of at the coming of Christ, and at the day of judgment. Follow the example that David sets you: he says, 'I am a companion of all who fear you, of those who keep your precepts.'[149] Remember the words of Solomon: 'Whoever walks with the wise becomes wise, but the companion of fools will suffer harm.'[150] Depend on it, keeping bad company in your life here and now is the sure way to get worse company in the life to come.

---

147   2 Chronicles 18:1
148   Proverbs 18:22
149   Psalm 119:63
150   Proverbs 13:20

4. SPECIAL RULES FOR YOUNG MEN

Lastly, I will set down some particular rules of behaviour, which I strongly advise all young men to follow.

RESOLVE AT ONCE TO RENOUNCE EVERY KNOWN SIN, HOWEVER SMALL

First, resolve at once, with God's help, to renounce every known sin, however small. Look within yourself, each one of you. Examine your own heart. Do you see there any habit or custom which you know to be wrong in God's sight? If you do, do not delay a moment in attacking it. Resolve at once to lay it aside.

Nothing darkens the judgment so much, nothing deadens the conscience so definitely, as *an allowed sin*. It may be a little one, but it is no less dangerous for all that. A small leak will sink a great ship, and a small spark will kindle a great fire, and a little allowed sin will ruin an immortal soul. Take my advice and never spare a little sin. Israel was commanded to slay every Canaanite, both great and small. Act on the same principle and show no mercy to little sins. The book of the Song of Solomon expresses it well: 'Catch the foxes for us, the little foxes that spoil the vineyards.'[151]

Be sure that no wicked man ever intended to be so wicked at the beginning. But he began with allowing himself some *little* misdemeanour; and that led on to something greater; and that, in time, produced something greater still; and, in this way, he became the miserable being that he is now. When the court official Hazael heard from Elisha about the horrible acts that he would commit in the future, he said with astonishment, 'What is your servant, who is but a dog, that he should do this great thing?'[152] But he allowed sin to take root in his heart; and, in the end, he did them all.

Young men, resist sin in its beginnings. They may look small and insignificant, but hear what I say: resist them, make no compromise, let no sin lodge quietly and undisturbed in your heart. 'The mother of mischief,' says an old proverb, 'is no bigger than a midge's wing.' There is nothing finer than the point of a needle, but when it has made a hole, it draws all the thread after it. Remember the apostle Paul's words, 'A little leaven (yeast) leavens the whole lump.'[153]

Many a young man could tell you with sorrow and shame that he traces the ruin of all his worldly prospects back to this point: to

---

151   Song of Solomon 2:15
152   2 Kings 8:13
153   1 Corinthians 5:6

giving way to sin in its beginnings. He began habits of falsehood and dishonesty in little things, and they grew. Step by step, he went from bad to worse, until he did things that, at one time, he would have thought impossible. Then at last, he has lost his way, lost his character, lost his comfort, and just about lost his soul. He allowed a gap in the wall of his conscience because it seemed a little one. But, once allowed, that gap grew larger every day until, at last, the whole wall seemed to come down.

Remember this especially in matters of *truth* and *honesty*. Be scrupulous about things of little value or importance. 'One who is faithful in a very little is also faithful in much.'[154] Whatever the world wants to say, there are no little sins. All great buildings are made up of little parts; the first stone is as important as any other. All habits are formed by a succession of little acts, and the first little act is of mighty consequence. Do you know the fable where an axe begs the trees to let him have one little piece of wood to make a handle, with the promise that he would never trouble them again? The axe got the handle that he asked for, and he soon cut all the trees down. The devil only wants to get the wedge of a little allowed sin into your heart, and you will soon be all his own. It is a wise saying of the English Puritan writer William Bridge: 'There is nothing small betwixt us and God, for God is an infinite God.'

There are two ways of coming down from the top of a church steeple; one is to jump down, and the other is to come down by the steps: both will lead you to the bottom. So, also, there are two

---

154   Luke 16:10

ways of going to hell; one is to walk into it with your eyes open: very few people do that. The other way is to go down by the steps of little sins: that way, I fear, is only too common.

If you put up with a few little sins, you will soon want a few more. Even as an unbeliever, Juvenal could say, 'Whoever was content with only one sin?'[155] Your path will be regularly worse and worse every year. Jeremy Taylor aptly described the progress of sin in a man: 'First it startles him, then it becomes pleasing, then easy, then delightful, then frequent, then habitual, then confirmed! Then the man is impenitent, then obstinate, then resolves never to repent, and then he is damned.'[156]

Young men, if you do not want to come to this, remember the rule I am giving you today: resolve at once to renounce every known sin.

RESOLVE TO SHUN EVERYTHING WHICH MAY PROVE AN OPPORTUNITY FOR SIN

Next, resolve, by God's help, to shun everything which may prove an occasion for sin. It is an excellent saying of good Bishop Joseph Hall, 'He that would be safe from the acts of evil, must widely avoid the occasions.'[157] There is an old fable where a butterfly once asked an owl how she should deal with the fire which had singed her wings. In reply, the owl advised her not even to look at its smoke.

---

155   Juvenal (34-12AD) was a Roman satirical poet.
156   Church of England minister, 1613-67.
157   Joseph Hall (1574-1656) was Anglican Bishop of Norwich

It is not enough that we resolve to commit no sin. We must carefully keep at a distance from all opportunities for it. This is how we assess our use of time, the books that we read, the families that we visit, the company we keep. We must not content ourselves with saying, 'There is nothing positively *wrong* here.' We must go further and ask, 'Is there anything here which may prove to be an opportunity for sin for me?'

This, remember, is one great reason why *laziness* is to be avoided so much. It is not that doing nothing is itself so positively wicked; it is the opportunity it gives for evil thoughts and fruitless day-dreaming; it is the wide door it opens for Satan to throw in the seeds of bad things; this is what is to be feared the most. If David had not given the devil an opportunity by lazing around on his housetop at Jerusalem, he would probably never have seen Bathsheba, nor murdered her husband Uriah.

This, too, is one of the great reasons why many *worldly amusements* are so objectionable. In some instances, it may be impossible to prove that they are inherently unscriptural and wrong. But there is little difficulty in showing that the *tendency* of almost all of them is most damaging to the soul. They sow the seeds of an earthly and sensual frame of mind. They war against the life of faith. They promote an unhealthy and unnatural craving after excitement. They minister to the lust of the flesh, and the lust of the eyes, and the pride of life.[158] They dim the view of heaven and eternity, and give a false colour to the things of today. They discourage the heart when it comes to private prayer, Bible reading

---

158   1 John 2:16

and calm communion with God. The man who engages in many worldly amusements is like one who gives Satan the advantage. He has a battle to fight, and he gives his enemy the benefit of sun, wind and hill. It would be strange indeed if he did not find himself continually defeated.

Young men, try as far as you can to keep clear of everything which may prove damaging to your soul. 'Never hold a candle to the devil', as the saying goes; do not help the devil in his work. People may say you are being over-scrupulous, too particular. They may ask where the harm is in doing such-and-such? But do not listen to them. It is dangerous to play tricks with sharp tools; it is far more dangerous to take liberties with your immortal soul. Anyone who wants to be safe must not go near the brink of danger. He must think of his heart as a barrel of gunpowder, and be careful not to handle one spark of temptation more than he can help.

What is the point of praying, 'Lead us not into temptation', unless you are yourselves careful not to run into it? Or praying 'deliver us from the evil one,' unless you show a desire to keep out of the devil's way?[159] Learn from Joseph's example: not only did he refuse his mistress' invitation to sin, but he showed his wise caution in refusing to even to be with her.[160] Take to heart Solomon's advice. Not only does he say: 'do not travel' on the path of wickedness – but he also says, 'Avoid it; do not go on it; turn away from it and pass on.'[161] Not only does he say not to get drunk, he

---

159   Matthew 6:13
160   Genesis 39:10
161   Proverbs 4:15

even says not to 'look at wine when it is red, when it sparkles in the cup and goes down smoothly!'[162] The man who took the Nazirite vow in Israel not only resolved to drink no wine, he even abstained from grapes in any shape whatsoever. Paul does not merely say not to do evil; he says: 'Abhor what is evil.'[163] 'Flee youthful passions,' he writes to Timothy; get as far away from them as possible.[164] Alas, how necessary cautions like this are! Dinah insisted on going out among the wicked people of Shechem to see their ways, and she lost her reputation. Lot insisted on pitching his tent near sinful Sodom, and he lost everything but his life.

Young men, be wise before it is too late. Do not always be trying to see how near you can allow the enemy of souls to come and still escape him. Hold him at arm's length. Try to keep clear of temptation as far as possible, and this will be one great way to keep clear of sin.

RESOLVE NEVER TO FORGET THE EYE OF GOD

The eye of God! Think of that. Everywhere, in every house, on every street, in every room, in every group of people, alone or in a crowd, the eye of God is always upon you. 'The eyes of the Lord are in every place, keeping watch on the evil and the good.'[165] And they are eyes that search hearts as well as actions.

---

162   Proverbs 23:31
163   Romans 12:9
164   2 Timothy 2:22
165   Proverbs 15:3

Try, I beg you all, to realise this fact. Remember that you are dealing with an all-seeing God, a God who neither slumbers nor sleeps.[166] A God who perceives your thoughts from afar, and with whom the night will shine like the day.[167] You may leave your father's house and go away like the prodigal son into a distant country.[168] You may think that there is nobody to watch your conduct; but the eye and ear of God are there before you. You may deceive your parents or employers; you may tell them lies, and be one thing before their faces and another behind their backs, but you cannot deceive God. He knows you through and through. He has heard everything you have said today. He knows what you are thinking about at this minute. He has set your most secret sins before his face; one day, to your shame, they will come out before the whole world unless you take care. Remember we have a God 'who will bring to light the things now hidden in darkness and will disclose the purposes of the heart.'[169]

How little this is really felt! How many things are done frequently, which men would never do if they thought they would be seen! How many matters are carried out in the chambers of the imagination, which would not stand the light of day! Yes; men think things in private, and say things in private, and do things in private which they would be ashamed and embarrassed to have exposed before the world. The sound of a footstep coming has stopped many a deed of wickedness. A knock at the door has caused many an evil work to be hastily suspended and hurriedly

---

166   Psalm 121:4
167   Psalm 139:2,12
168   Luke 15:13
169   1 Corinthians 4:5

laid aside. But what miserable drivelling foolishness this is! There is an all-seeing witness with us wherever we go. Lock the door, draw the curtains, shut the shutters, put out the light; it does not matter; it makes no difference. God is everywhere; you cannot shut him out, or prevent him seeing. 'And no creature is hidden from his sight, but all are naked and exposed to the eyes of him to whom we must give account.'[170] Young Joseph understood this completely when his mistress tempted him. There was no-one in the house to see them, no human eye to witness against him. But Joseph was a man who lived in the sight of him who is invisible: 'How then can I do sthis great wickedness,' he said, 'and sin against God?'[171]

Young men, I ask you all to read Psalm 139. I advise you all to learn it by heart. Make it the test of everything you do in this world. Say to yourself often, 'Do I remember that God sees me?'

Live in the sight of God. This is what Abraham did; he walked *before* God. This is what Enoch did; he walked *with* God. This is what heaven itself will be, the eternal presence of God. Do nothing you would not like God to see. Say nothing you would not like God to hear. Write nothing you would not like God to read. Go to no place where you would not like God to find you. Read no book of which you would not like God to say, 'Show it me.' Never spend your time in such a way that you would not like to have God say, 'What are you doing?'

---

170   Hebrews 4:13
171   Genesis 39:9

BE CONSCIENTIOUS ABOUT
USING OF MEANS OF GRACE

I have in mind the ways in which God brings salvation and blessing to his people, such as the preaching of the word, Bible reading
and Bible study, prayer, baptism, the Lord's Supper, and godly
fellowship with other Christians. And I want to urge you to be
regular in going to God's house whenever it is open for prayer and
preaching and it is in your power to attend. Be regular in keeping
the Lord's day holy, and resolve that the Lord's day will always be
given to its rightful owner.

I do not want to leave any false impression on your minds.
Do not go away and say I told you that going to church is what
makes you a Christian. I tell you no such thing. I have no wish to
see you grow up like the Pharisees, wedded to the externals of religion. If you think that simply taking yourself to a certain place,
at a certain time, on a certain day in the week, will make you a
Christian and prepare you to meet God, I tell you emphatically
you are miserably deceived. Service done without the heart is un-
profitable and useless. True worshippers are those who 'worship
the Father in spirit and truth, for the Father is seeking such people
to worship him.'[172]

But means of grace are not to be despised just because they
cannot save you. Gold is not food; you cannot eat it, but you
would not therefore say it is useless and throw it away. Your soul's
eternal well-being most certainly does not depend on means of
grace but, without them, it is certain that your soul will generally

172   John 4:23

not do well. God *could* take all those who are saved to heaven in a chariot of fire (as he did with Elijah), but he does not do so.[173] He *could* teach all his people by visions, dreams and miraculous interventions, without requiring them to read or think for themselves, but he does not do so. And why not? Because he is a God that works by *means*, and it is his rule and will that in all our dealings with him, *means* shall be used. Only a fool or fanatic would think of building a house without ladders and scaffolding, and no wise man will despise means of grace.

I will dwell on this point a while longer because Satan will try hard to fill your minds with arguments against means of grace. He will draw your attention to the numbers of people who make use of them and are no better for it. 'See there,' he will whisper, 'don't you see how those who go to church are no better than those who stay away?' But do not let this influence you. It is never fair to argue against a thing because it is used inappropriately. It does not follow that means of grace can do no good because some people get no good from them. Medicine is not to be despised because some take it and do not recover their health. No-one would think of giving up eating and drinking because others choose to eat and drink inappropriately, and so make themselves ill. The value of means of grace, like other things, depends largely on the way and the spirit in which we use them.

---

173   2 Kings 2:11

PREACHING OF THE GOSPEL

I dwell on this point, too, because I am very anxious that every young man should regularly hear the preaching of Christ's gospel. I cannot tell you how important I think this is. By God's blessing, the ministry of the gospel might be the means of converting your soul, of leading you to a saving knowledge of Christ, of making you a child of God in deed and in truth. This would certainly be cause for eternal thankfulness! This would be an event which would make the angels would rejoice.

But even if this were not the case, there is a restraining power and influence in the ministry of the gospel, under which I earnestly desire every young man to be brought. There are thousands who are kept back from evil by hearing the word of God preached, although it may not yet have turned them to God. It has made them far better members of society, even though it has not yet made them true Christians. There is a certain kind of mysterious power in the faithful preaching of the gospel; it imperceptibly works on the many people who listen to it without receiving it into their hearts. To hear sin condemned and holiness encouraged, to hear Christ exalted and the works of the devil denounced, to hear the kingdom of heaven and its blessedness described, and the world and its emptiness exposed; to hear this week after week, Sunday after Sunday, is seldom without good effect to the soul. It makes it far harder to run into excess and extravagance straight afterwards. It acts as a wholesome check upon a person's heart. This, I believe, is one way in which God keeps this promise: 'My word... shall not return to me empty.'[174] There is much truth in that excellent saying of George Whitefield, 'The gospel keeps many a one from the gaol and gallows, if it does not keep him from hell.'

THE LORD'S DAY

Let me here name another point which is closely connected with this subject. Let nothing ever tempt you to become a Sabbath-breaker. I urgently bring this to your attention. Make it a matter of conscience to give all your Sundays to God. Give yourself to worship, to fellowship with God's people, prayer, rest, and to Bible reading and study. A spirit of disregard for this holy day is growing up among us with fearful rapidity, and not least among young men. Sunday travelling, Sunday visiting, Sunday excursions and the like are becoming more common every year, and they are doing infinite harm to souls.

Young men, be cautious on this point. Whether you live in the town or country, have a decided habit; resolve not to misuse your Sabbath. Do not let the plausible excuse of 'necessary relaxation', or the example of everyone around you, or the invitation of friends you may be thrown together with. Let none of these things move you to abandon this settled rule: that God's day will be given to God.

Once you stop caring about Sundays, you will eventually stop caring for your soul. The steps which lead to this outcome are easy and unremarkable. If you begin not honouring God's day, you will soon stop honouring God's house. If you stop honouring

---

174   Isaiah 55:11

God's house, you will soon stop honouring God's book. If you stop honouring God's book, you will soon give God no honour at all. Once someone lays the foundation stone of having no Sabbath, I am never surprised if he finishes with the top-stone of no God. Judge Hale made this remarkable observation: of all the people who were convicted of capital crimes while he was upon the bench, he found only a few who had not started their career of wickedness by neglecting the Sabbath.[175]

Young men, you may be thrown among companions who forget the honour of the Lord's day, but resolve, by God's help, that you will always remember to keep it holy. Honour it by a regular attendance at some place where the gospel is preached. Settle down under a faithful ministry and, once settled, let your place in church never be empty. Believe me, you will find a special blessing following you:

> If you turn back your foot from the Sabbath, from doing your pleasure on my holy day, and call the Sabbath a delight and the holy day of the Lord honorable; if you honor it, not going your own ways, or seeking your own pleasure, or talking idly; then you shall take delight in the Lord, and I will make you ride on the heights of the earth; I will feed you with the heritage of Jacob your father, for the mouth of the Lord has spoken.[176]

---

175   Sir Matthew Hale (1609-76) was an English jurist and writer. Capital crimes were those punishable by death.
176   Isaiah 58:13-14

And one thing is very certain: your feelings about the Sabbath will always be a test and criterion of your fitness for heaven. Sabbaths are a foretaste and fragment of heaven. The person who finds them a burden and not a privilege may be sure that their heart is in need of a mighty change.

RESOLVE THAT WHEREVER YOU ARE, YOU WILL PRAY

Prayer is the life-breath of a man's soul. We may have a name for being a Christian and be counted as a Christian but, without prayer, we are dead in the sight of God. The feeling that we must cry to God for mercy and peace is a mark of grace. The habit of laying before him all our soul's needs is evidence that we have the Spirit of adoption. And prayer is the way that God has appointed for us to receive the relief of our spiritual necessities; it opens the treasure-chest; it sets the fountain flowing. If we do not have, it is because we do not ask.

Prayer is the way to receive the outpouring of the Spirit upon our hearts. Jesus has promised the Holy Spirit, the Comforter. He is ready to come with all his precious gifts, renewing, sanctifying, purifying, strengthening, cheering, encouraging, enlightening, teaching, directing, guiding into all truth. But he waits for us to plead with him.

Here it is—and I say this with sorrow—here it is that men fall short so miserably. There are few who pray, many who go down on their knees and say a form of prayer perhaps, but few who pray. Few who cry to God, few who call upon the Lord, few who seek as if they wanted to find, few who knock as if they hungered and thirsted, few who wrestle, few who strive with God earnestly for an answer, few who will give him no rest, few who continue in prayer, few who are watchful about prayer, few who always pray without ceasing and do not give up. Yes, few pray! Prayer is one of those things that is assumed as a matter of course, but seldom practised. It is something which is everybody's business, but something that hardly anybody actually does.

Young men, believe me, if your soul is to be saved, you must pray. God has no children who do not speak. If you are to resist the world, the flesh and the devil, you must pray.[177] It is useless to look for strength in the hour of trial, if you have not asked for it beforehand. You may be thrown together with people who never pray; you may have to sleep in accommodation with someone who never asks anything of God. Still, mark my words: *you must pray.*

I can quite believe you find great difficulties with prayer—difficulties with finding opportunities, times and places. I do not want to be too prescriptive about these things. I leave them to your own conscience. You must be guided by circumstances. Our Lord Jesus Christ prayed on a mountain; Isaac prayed in the fields; Hezekiah turned his face to the wall as he lay upon his bed; Daniel prayed by the riverside; the apostle Peter prayed on the housetop. I have heard of young men praying in stables and haylofts. All that I argue for is this: you must know what it is to 'go into your room … and prayer to your Father, who is in secret.'[178] There must be

177   1 John 2:16
178   Matthew 6:6

defined times when you speak to God face to face; you must have
your time of prayer every day. *You must pray.*

Without prayer, any advice or instruction is useless. Prayer is
the last item that Paul lists in his pieces of spiritual armour in
Ephesians 6 but, in truth, it is first in value and importance. It is
the food which you must eat every day if you want to travel safely
through the wilderness of this life. It is only in the strength of
prayer that you will make your way towards the mount of God. I
have heard it said that the needle-grinders of Sheffield sometimes
wore a magnetic mouthpiece when they were working; it caught
all the fine metal dust that flew around them, preventing it en-
tering their lungs, and so saving their lives. Prayer is the 'mouthpiece' that you must wear continually, or else you will never work
uninjured by the unhealthy atmosphere of this sinful world. *You
must pray.*

Young men, be certain of this: no time is so well spent as that
which spent on your knees. Make time for it, whatever your job
may be. Think of David, king of Israel: what does he say? 'Evening
and morning and at noon I utter my complaint and moan, and
he hears my voice.'[179] Think of Daniel. He had all the business of
a kingdom on his hands; yet he prayed three times a day.[180] That
was the secret of his safety in wicked Babylon. Think of Solomon.
He began his reign with prayer for help and assistance, and en-
joyed wonderful prosperity.[181] Think of Nehemiah. He could find
time to pray to the God of heaven even when he was standing in

---

179   Psalm 55:17
180   Daniel 6:10
181   1 Kings 8:22

the presence of his master, Artaxerxes.[182] Think of the example these godly men have left you, and go and do likewise.

I long that the Lord may give all of you the spirit of grace and prayer! I would gladly agree to the contents of this little book being entirely forgotten, if the importance of prayer might be deeply impressed on your hearts.

---

182   Nehemiah 2:4

5. CONCLUSION: ARE THESE THINGS TRUE?

And now I hasten towards a conclusion. I have said things that some people may not like, and not accept; but I appeal to your conscience: *are they not true?*

Young men, you all have consciences. Even though we are corrupt and ruined by the Fall, each of us has a conscience. In a corner of each heart, there sits a witness for God, a 'small voice' who declares us guilty when we do wrong and approves when we do right. To that witness, I make my appeal: the things that I have been saying are true, are they not?

Go then, young men, and be determined to remember your Creator in the days of your youth.[183] Before the day of grace is past; before your conscience has become hardened by age and deadened by repeated trampling under foot; while you have strength, time and opportunity; go and join yourself to the Lord in an everlasting covenant not to be forgotten. The Holy Spirit will not contend with us for ever. The voice of conscience will become feebler and fainter every year that you continue to resist it. The Athenians said to Paul, 'We want to hear you again about this'—but, in fact, they had heard him for the last time.[184] Make haste and do not delay. Do not linger or hesitate anymore.

COMFORT TO OTHERS

Think of the unspeakable comfort you will give to parents, relations and friends, if you take my advice. They have spent time, money and health to bring you up and help make you what you are. Surely, they deserve some consideration on your part. Who can calculate the joy and gladness which young people are able to bring about? Who can express the anxiety and sorrow that sons like Esau, Hophni and Phinehas, and Absalom can cause?[185] Solomon is right to say, 'A wise son makes a glad father, but a foolish son is a sorrow to his mother'[186] Please consider these things and give God your heart! Let it not be said of you (as it is of many) that your youth was a blunder, your manhood a struggle, and your old age a regret.[187]

INSTRUMENTS OF DOING GOOD

Think of the good you could achieve as the instrument of doing good to the world. Almost all the most eminent saints of God turned to the Lord early. Moses, Samuel, David and Daniel all

---

184   Acts 17:32
185   Genesis 25-27; 1 Samuel 1-4; 2 Samuel 13
186   Proverbs 10:1
187   Benjamin Disraeli

served God from their youth. God seems to delight in putting special honour upon young servants. Remember the honour he placed upon the young king, Edward VI. If young men in our own day would devote the springtime of their lives to God, what results might we confidently expect? Workers are needed now, for almost every great and good cause but they cannot be found. There are mechanisms of every kind for spreading God's truth but there are not enough willing hands to use them. It is easier to raise the *money* for doing good. than it is to raise the *men*. Ministers are wanted for new churches; missionaries are wanted for new overseas opportunities; workers are wanted for neglected districts; teachers are wanted for new schools. Many a good cause is standing still merely for want of men! The supply of godly, faithful, trustworthy men for positions such as these is far below the demand.

Young men of the present day, you are wanted for God. This is an age of particular activity. We are shaking off some of our past selfishness. Men no longer sleep the sleep of apathy and indifference about others, as their forefathers did. They are beginning to be ashamed of thinking like Cain, 'Am I my brother's keeper?'[188] A wide field of usefulness is open before you, if you are only willing to enter it. The harvest is great but the labourers are few.[189] Be keen to do good works. Come and serve the Lord's cause against the mighty. This is to be like God in some way: not only good, but doing good.[190] This is the way to follow the steps of your Lord

---

188   Genesis 4:9
189   Luke 10:2
190   Psalm 119:68

and Saviour: 'he went about doing good.'[191] This is to live as David did: he 'served the purpose of God in his own generation.'[192]

There is no doubt that this is the path which most fitting for an immortal soul. Would you not rather leave this world like Josiah, lamented by all; rather than depart like Jehoram, 'with no-one's regret'?[193] Which is it better: to be an idle, frivolous, useless consumer, to live for your body, your selfishness, your lusts and your pride; or to spend and be spent in the glorious cause of being useful to your fellow human beings? To be like William Wilberforce or Lord Shaftesbury—a blessing to your country and the world; to be like John Howard—the friend of the prisoner and the captive; to be like Christian Schwartz—the spiritual father of hundreds of immortal souls in far-off nations; to be like that man of God, Robert M'Cheyne—a burning and a shining light, a living letter from Christ, known and read by all men, the reviver of many a Christian heart?[194] Who can doubt the best path? Who can, for one moment, doubt?

---

191   Acts 10:38
192   Acts 13:36
193   2 Chronicles 21:20
194   William Wilberforce (1759-1833) was an English statesman and philanthropist. He laboured to abolish the slave trade among the English and died one month before the legislation passed Parliament officially ending slavery in all the English colonies. Anthony Shaftesbury (1801-85) was a man of God who was committed to reforming many inhumane practices in England. John Howard (1726-90) was an English philanthropist and advocate of prison reform; he devoted his life to exposing and improving horribly inhumane conditions in the prisons. Christian F. Schwartz (1726-98) was a German missionary to southern India whose labours over 40 years saw the establishment of many schools and congregations. Robert Murray M'Cheyne (1813-43) was Scottish pastor known as one of the godliest men of the 19th century.

Young men, think about your responsibilities. Think of the privilege and luxury of doing good. Decide today that you will be useful. And, at once, give your hearts to Christ.

HAPPINESS TO YOUR OWN SOUL

Lastly, think of the happiness that will come to your own soul if you serve God; happiness as you travel through life, and happiness in the end when the journey is over. Believe me, whatever misleading ideas you may have heard, believe me, there is a reward for the righteous even in this world. Godliness has rewards in *this* life, as well as in the world to come. There is a solid peace in feeling that God is your friend. There is a real satisfaction in knowing that, however unworthy you are, you are complete in Christ; that you have an enduring inheritance; that you have chosen what is better, and it will not be taken from you.

As Proverbs reminds us, the faithless will be fully repaid for his own ways, but a good man will be fully rewarded for his.[195] The path of the worldly man grows darker and darker every year that he lives; the path of the Christian is like a shining light, brighter and brighter to the very end. His sun is just rising when the sun of the worldly is setting forever; his best things are all beginning to blossom and bloom forever, when the things of the worldly man are all slipping out of his hands and passing away.

Young men, these things are true. Take to heart these words of encouragement and exhortation. Be persuaded. Take up the cross. Follow Christ. Surrender yourselves to God!

---

195   Proverbs 14:14

This short book was written many years ago – but its message remains as relevant as ever. The author is concerned for **YOUNG MEN**, as he feels that they need particular encouragement and instruction. His 'Thoughts for Young Men' are timeless. If you are a young man, read them and take them to heart. If you are a parent, relation or friend of a young man, read it, and pass it on.

The author presents his material with his typical gentleness, humility, clarity, encouragement and a striking lack of guilt-trips! Read and be inspired to grow in your relationship with our Lord Jesus Christ.

This edition takes Ryle's very beautiful 19th century prose and revises it slightly to make it more accessible to 21st century readers. If you would like to read it in his original words, it is available free online: www.chapellibrary.org/files/6413/7643/3390/tfym.pdf